At Work in a Museum

written by Robin Bromley
illustrated by Arvis Stewart

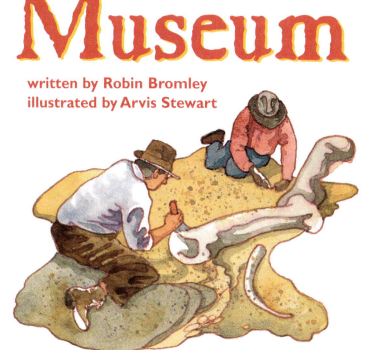

SCHOLASTIC INC.
New York   Toronto   London   Auckland   Sydney
Mexico City   New Delhi   Hong Kong   Buenos Aires

No part of this publication may be reproduced in whole or in part, or stored in a retrieval system, or transmitted in any form or by any means, electronic, mechanical, photocopying, recording, or otherwise, without written permission of the publisher. For information regarding permission, write to Scholastic Inc., Education Group, 555 Broadway, New York, NY 10012.

Developed by Kirchoff/Wohlberg, Inc., in cooperation with Scholastic Inc.

Copyright © 2002 by Scholastic Inc.
All rights reserved.   Published by Scholastic Inc.   Printed in the U.S.A.
ISBN 0-439-35110-3
SCHOLASTIC and associated logos and designs are trademarks
and/or registered trademarks of Scholastic Inc.

9 10 11   40   14 13 12

There are many kinds of museums. Visit one, and you will see mummies, crowns, or suits of armor. In another, you will see paintings, statues, or a famous baseball player's bat.

There are also all kinds of work for people to do in museums. This book is about people who help create dinosaur displays at natural history museums.

You've probably seen pictures or models of dinosaurs. Perhaps you've been to a museum and seen some yourself. But dinosaurs have been dead for 65 million years. How did they get into a modern museum?

Dinosaurs died long ago, but they didn't completely disappear. They left footprints in the mud and sand that slowly turned into stone. Some of their bones were trapped in rock.

These prints and bones are called fossils. Many stay buried for millions of years. About 175 years ago, people began finding fossils and learning more about them.

Mary Ann Mantell discovered one of the first fossils in England in 1822. A few years later, the British scientist Richard Owen gave them a name—*dinosauria*. It means "terrible lizards." Scientists who look for fossils are called *paleontologists*. They study these very old animals and plants.

One famous paleontologist was Roy Chapman Andrews. He searched for dinosaurs in the Gobi Desert of Mongolia. In 1922, Andrews made an important discovery. He found a huge number of dinosaur skeletons in the hard desert sand.

Scientists still find fossils in the Gobi Desert. Paleontologists are discovering dinosaurs in other parts of the world too. In the Sahara Desert, close to Nigeria, scientists recently found kinds of dinosaurs no one had ever seen before. In the United States, museum workers found the most complete skeleton of T. rex ever. They named it Sue. It's now in a museum in Chicago, Illinois.

How do people find the bones of animals that died millions of years ago? What do they do with their fossil discoveries?

Most fossils are found by a team of workers. Paleontologists lead the group. Other team members may be geologists, who know about the history of the Earth and the age of rocks. Artists and photographers go to make videos or pictures of the site and the fossils. Field assistants measure fossils and dig them very carefully out of rock.

The team drives into an area like the Gobi Desert and sets up their tents. Then they hike around sand dunes, cliffs, old riverbeds, or quarries looking for tracks and bones.

Once they find something, they brush away the sand and loose rock. They dig a ditch around the item. Workers brush the delicate fossil with shellac so it won't break. Then they cover it with wet newspaper and wrap it in cloth strips dipped in plaster. The plaster hardens and creates a cast. The cast protects the fossil.

   Paleontologists pack the fossil in straw, put it in a box, and ship it home. They save all the small pieces too. They carefully label each one. That way they will know where it goes when they try to put the skeleton together.

   Back at the museum, workers called "preparators" gently remove the fossil from its crate. They saw off the plaster. Then they use chisels, saws, and other tools to carefully free the fragile bones.

Geologists study fossils with high-powered scanning tools. Their discoveries raise exciting questions. One time, scientists found the hip bone of a Triceratops with T. rex teethmarks in it. It made them wonder how hard a T. rex could bite. To find out, they put a model tooth in a drill. They measured how hard a bite would have to be to make the same holes in a similar bone. They learned a T. rex's bite was much stronger than a lion's.

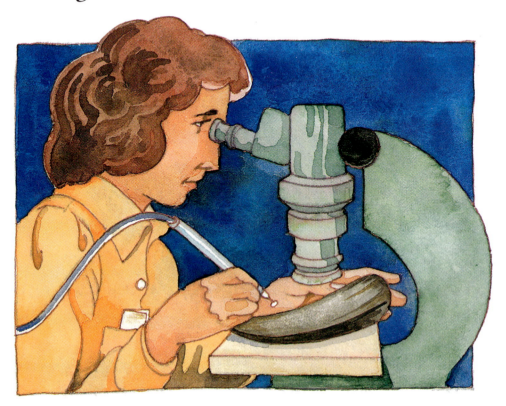

Other mysteries are harder to solve. Scientists still don't know whether T. rex lived alone or with a family. The discovery of Sue shows that if T. rex did live in groups, it didn't live peacefully. Sue's skull was full of T. rex bite marks.

Discoveries can also change scientists' ideas. They used to think oviraptors stole eggs from other animals because they were found on nests. When they discovered the eggs were an oviraptor's eggs, they realized oviraptors didn't steal eggs. They hatched them.

When they want to put a skeleton together, museum workers first build a frame. Then they string a wire through every bone and attach it by hand to other bones and the frame. If a piece is missing, they replace it with a fiberglass bone.

To make a fiberglass bone, artists cover a real bone with rubber. When the rubber dries, they peel it off. This leaves a mold, which they fill with fiberglass. The hard fiberglass looks like a real bone. Museums that don't have fossils show fiberglass copies.

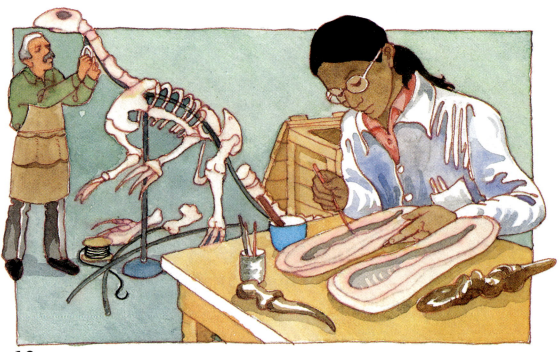

Artists and scientists usually work together to set up exhibits. Take a display of dinosaurs from the Gobi, for instance. The scientists ask an artist to create a model of a dinosaur with leathery skin and feathers.

Artists also paint scenery showing where dinosaurs lived, what they ate, and animals they lived with.

Media artists put together maps, videos, and special computer programs to go with the exhibit. These explain where the fossils were found and tell what is known about them.

Media artists also create websites that show how much a museum has to offer. In addition to exhibits, many museums have arts and science workshops for teachers, families, and children. Some show films and host special events. There are libraries for scientists, tours to faraway places, and summer camps. Museum editors also publish magazines and newspapers for children and adults.

From the guides and guards you see in the museum hallway to secretaries, cooks, and mechanics behind the scenes, lots of people work together to make each trip to a museum an adventure.

What kind of work do you think you would you like to do in the future? Build a website? Manage a store? Hunt for dinosaurs? Chances are, you could do it in a museum.